Coral Reefs

by Susan H. Gray

Content Adviser: Terrence E. Young Jr., M.Ed., M.L.S.,
Jefferson Parish (La.) Public Schools

Reading Adviser: Dr. Linda D. Labbo, Department of Reading
Education, College of Education,
The University of Georgia

COMPASS POINT BOOKS

Minneapolis, Minnesota

FIRST REPORTS

Compass Point Books
3722 West 50th Street, #115
Minneapolis, MN 55410

Visit Compass Point Books on the Internet at *www.compasspointbooks.com* or e-mail your request
to *custserv@compasspointbooks.com*

Photographs ©: International Stock/Beverly Factor, cover; Index Stock Imagery, 4; Visuals Unlimited/Hal Beral, 5; Visuals
Unlimited/Paul Averbach, 6; Christian Michaels/FPG International, 7; Brian Parker/Tom Stack and Associates, 8; Visuals
Unlimited/John D. Cunningham, 9; Harvey Lloyd/FPG International, 10; Visuals Unlimited/David M. Phillips, 11 top; Visuals
Unlimited/Marty Snyderman, 11 bottom; Keith Gillett/Tom Stack and Associates, 12; Wayne Levin/FPG International, 13; Visuals
Unlimited/Martin G. Miller, 14; Index Stock Imagery, 15, 16; Josef Beck/FPG International, 17; Photo Network/Hal Beral, 18;
Visuals Unlimited/David B. Fleetham, 19 top; Brian Parker/Tom Stack and Associates, 19 bottom; International Stock/Beverly
Factor, 20; Karl and Jill Wallin/FPG International, 21; International Stock/Jeff Rotman, 22 top; Photo Network/Hal Beral, 22 bot-
tom; Visuals Unlimited/David B. Fleetham, 23; Unicorn Stock Photos/Abbey Sea Photography, 24; Carl Roessler/FPG
International, 25; Photo Network/Hal Beral, 26; Visuals Unlimited/John D. Cunningham, 27; David Fleetham/FPG International,
28; Mark Stack/Tom Stack and Associates, 29 top; David B. Fleetham/Tom Stack and Associates, 29 bottom; Visuals
Unlimited/David B. Fleetham, 30; Norbert Wu, 31; David B. Fleetham/Tom Stack and Associates, 32; Photo Network/Hal Beral,
33; Tom and Therisa Stack/Tom Stack and Associates, 35; Visual Unlimited/Glenn M. Oliver, 37; Index Stock Imagery, 38; Visuals
Unlimited/L. Linkhart, 39; Tom Stack/Tom Stack and Associates, 41; Tom and Therisa Stack/Tom Stack and Associates, 42.

Editors: E. Russell Primm and Emily J. Dolbear
Photo Researcher: Svetlana Zhurkina
Photo Selector: Dawn Friedman
Design: Bradfordesign, Inc.

Library of Congress Cataloging-in-Publication Data
Gray, Susan Heinrichs.
    Coral reefs / by Susan H. Gray.
        p. cm. — (First reports)
    Includes bibliographical references (p.   ) and index.
    Summary: Describes the physical features of a coral reef, its community of plants and animals,
    and environmental threats.
    ISBN 0-7565-0018-4 (hardcover : lib. bdg.)
        1. Coral reef ecology—Juvenile literature. 2. Coral reefs and islands—Juvenile literature.
    [1. Coral reef ecology. 2. Ecology. 3. Coral reefs and islands.] I. Title. II. Series.
    QH541.5.C7 G72 2000
    577.7'89—dc21   00-008528

Table of Contents

Where in the World?

▲ *Ant Atoll, a coral reef, in Micronesia*

Where in the world would you find animals building islands? Or animals with plants living in their bodies? Where would you see an animal squeezing its

▲ *The chestnut cowry, a snail with a shiny shell*

stomach out through its mouth? Or snails so lovely that people use them for jewelry? You can find all these things on **coral reefs**.

Coral reefs are underwater structures formed by animals. They are found only in the Pacific, Atlantic, and Indian Oceans. In some places, coral reefs stick up above the water's surface.

How can animals build such things? If you saw a reef far away, you might think it was a large rock. But up close, you would see tiny animals covering it. These animals are busy building the reef.

▲ *A boat looks tiny next to a part of the Great Barrier Reef in Australia*

Coral Animals

▲ Coral polyps

Coral animals are called **polyps**. A polyp is soft and small. Its body is a short tube with **tentacles** at the top. Tentacles are long, flexible structures at the mouth or head of an animal.

Sometimes a little bump forms on the polyp. It grows larger and larger and becomes a new polyp. This process is called **budding**. Each new polyp forms a cup around itself. The new cup attaches to the cup of the first polyp. So new polyps and their cups cover up old ones. The old polyps die, and the new polyps stack up higher and wider.

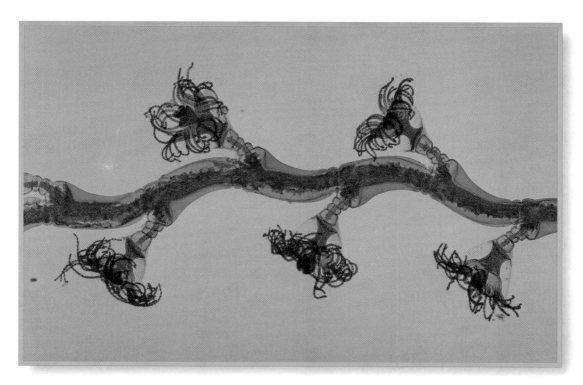

▲ *Polyps budding*

A very large group of polyps and cups is called a reef. Many reefs lie in the ocean near the tip of Florida. Scientists think it took thousands of years for these reefs to form.

▲ Coral reefs near Key West, Florida

How Do Polyps Eat?

Coral animals, or polyps, use their tentacles to catch food. Sometimes a polyp poisons its victim by stinging it. Then the tentacles move the victim into the polyp's mouth. Tiny animals called **zooplankton** float in the water around the reefs. Polyps love to eat zooplankton.

◀ *Zooplankton magnified 25 times*

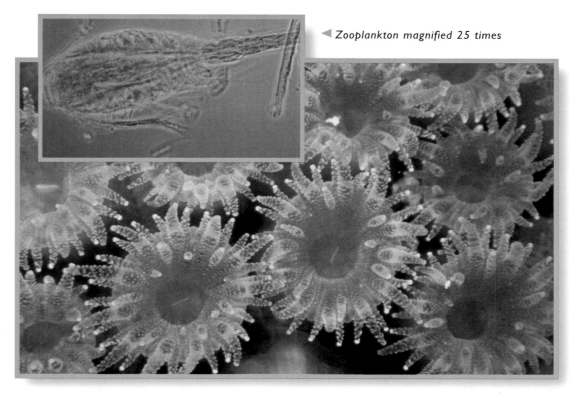

▲ *Star coral polyps feeding*

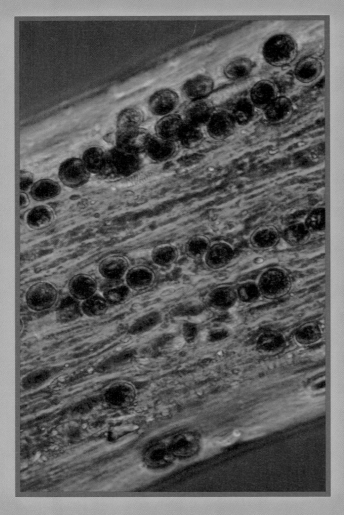

▲ *Algae living inside a coral polyp*

Polyps get food another way. Tiny plants called **algae** live inside the polyp. Sunlight shines down into the water and helps the algae to grow. As it grows, it becomes food for the polyp—so a polyp grows its own food right inside its body!

Reefs cannot form in the dark because algae need sunlight. They form in clear shallow water less than 250 feet (76 meters) deep. And reefs are found only in warm water. Almost all the world's reefs lie near the

equator—an imaginary line around the middle of the earth. Here, the conditions are best to support coral life.

▲ *A family explores a coral reef close to the surface.*

Types of Coral Reefs

▲ *A fringing reef in the Grand Cayman Islands*

There are three kinds of reefs. The first kind is a **fringing reef**. This reef extends from the shore into the sea. Sometimes there is a narrow stretch of water between the land and a fringing reef.

These reefs are found in many places. Some are just off the shores of Mexico, Cuba, and Central America.

The second kind of reef is a **barrier reef**. It may form several miles out from shore. A barrier reef creates a barrier between the land and the sea.

The largest barrier reef in the world is a chain of reefs near Australia. It is called the Great Barrier Reef.

▲ *The Great Barrier Reef in Australia*

It is more than 1,250 miles (2,012 kilometers) long! It is made up of about 2,500 small reefs and coral islands. They have names like Wreck Reef, Rooda Reef, Snake Reef, and Oom Reef.

The third kind of reef is an **atoll**. It is shaped like a ring and lies in the open sea. Many atolls are

▲ *Atolls*

very small. Others are big enough for people to live on.

A whole group of atolls lie near the tip of India. They are called the Maldives. These atolls are so large that cities are built on them. Other well-known atolls are Bikini Atoll and some of the Fiji islands.

▲ *A vacation resort in the Maldives*

Life around a Reef

Thousands of kinds of animals live in and around reefs. Reefs come in all kinds of shapes. Some look

▲ *Many kinds of coral are found in coral reefs.*

▲ Red whip coral

Elkhorn coral ▶

like bundles of pipes.
Others look like fingers,
antlers, or feathers.

▲ Cardinal soldierfish swim through a coral reef in Mexico.

Many animals find safety in a coral reef. They hide in its shadows and cracks. The sponge is one example. Sponges are simple animals with bodies full of holes. As water moves through them, they filter out the food they need. Sponges attach to something

▲ *Orange rope sponges*

solid and stay there for life. Many fish like to eat sponges, but sponges are safe in the reef's cracks.

◀ *A diver looks into a giant netted barrel sponge.*

▲ *A purple tube sponge*

Small fish also stay safely within the reef's cracks. Others swim freely, eating zooplankton and polyps. The parrot fish uses its hard beak to bite off chunks of coral. It grinds everything up in its throat. Then the parrot fish swallows the polyps and spits out the hard bits.

▲ *A parrot fish*

Moray eels lie hidden in the reef's cracks in the daytime. Then they slither around the reef at night. They have smooth, powerful bodies and mouths full of sharp teeth. They look like huge, strong snakes, but they are actually fish.

▲ A spotted moray eel

▲ A gray reef shark

Gray reef sharks also circle reefs. They can tell where other fish are by sensing their movements in the water.

Sea anemones are animals that attach to corals. They have short, stinging tentacles. A poison thread is coiled inside. When a small fish swims by, the

▲ Clown anemonefish swim safely through sea anemones.

poison threads shoot out and paralyze it. Then tentacles draw the helpless fish into the anemone's mouth.

▲ *A sea anemone eating a fish*

Crawling on the Reef

▲ *A starfish*

Many kinds of animals crawl around on the reef.
Snails, crabs, and starfish live there. Colorful snails
and slugs creep along, eating up dead plants and
animals. The snails called cowries have glossy shells.

▲ A flamingo tongue cowry
from Florida

A mole cowry from Hawaii ▶

People collect them and string them into necklaces and bracelets. Some cowries are even used as money! Hermit crabs also help clean up the area. They find empty snail shells to live in. Sometimes sponges or sea anemones already live on the outside of these shells. They travel wherever the hermit crab goes. In this way, they keep finding new food supplies.

▲ *A hermit crab with anemones on its shell*

Starfish also move about the reef, eating polyps and small clams. When a starfish is ready to eat, it shoves its stomach out through its mouth. The stomach covers the food and softens it with its own juices. Then the starfish draws the food into its stomach and pulls the stomach back in.

▲ *A bat starfish eating a sea urchin*

Starfish have a great way to survive. If a starfish loses an arm to a biting fish, it just grows a new one! Some kinds of starfish can grow a whole new body from a little piece of arm.

One of the starfish's favorite foods is clam—but they stay away from the giant clam. This animal grows up to 500 pounds (227 kilograms). Its giant shell is often covered with different corals.

▲ A diver near a Tridacna giant clam

Living as a Team

Sometimes animals and plants live together as a team. Both members of the team benefit from the relationship. This is called **symbiosis**.

▲ *Bridled cardinalfish hide in a sea anemone*

For example, a hermit crab may carry an anemone on its shell. The anemone gets to ride around to new food sources—and the hermit crab is safe from the bites of little fish. This is good for both members of the team.

The coral polyps and their algae are another team. The algae make food for the polyps, and the polyps give the algae a place to live. They also protect the algae from harsh sunlight.

Coral Bleaching

In the 1980s, many coral reefs began turning deathly white. People said the white reefs were "bleached."

▲ *A "bleached" brain coral*

Scientists found that the polyps in the reef no longer had algae in them. Polyps lose their algae when the seawater is too salty or too warm. The waters around the bleached reefs were warmer than normal due to several years of unusual weather. Some bleached reefs have started to recover, but it can take a long time.

Hurting the Reefs

Coral reefs are sensitive natural structures. Many things in the natural world can hurt the coral reefs. One such enemy is a huge starfish called the crown of thorns. It may have more than twenty arms, all covered with sharp spines. In one day, a crown of thorns

▲ *Crown of thorns starfish*

starfish can eat all the polyps in an area the size of a dollar bill. It leaves their empty cups behind and moves on. Scientists are working on ways to save the reefs from this hungry animal.

Typhoons and storms can also cause damage. Their winds and pounding waves break off chunks of coral. Animals hiding in those chunks are no longer protected.

▲ *A typhoon wave in Japan*

Threats from Humans

▲ Pollution from factories pours into the sea.

The biggest threats come from humans, however. Cities dump sewage, and factories pour wastes into the oceans. These pollute the water around reefs.

Suddenly, small things that live on sewage are everywhere. They are called bacteria. Bacteria use up so much oxygen that many animals aren't able to breathe.

Pollution also darkens the water. Then sunlight can't get through, and algae die inside the polyps. Then the polyps die. When the polyps disappear, the animals that feed on them die too.

Many tourists come to see coral reefs. They may just want to look and take pictures, but sometimes their boats knock off whole sections of the reefs. Some tourists break off pieces to take home. Others do not know they are killing polyps just by standing on the reefs.

Cyanide fishing is terrible for reefs too. Some fishers in the South Pacific put a deadly poison called cyanide in squirt bottles. Then they dive underwater and squirt it into cracks in the reefs. The poison stuns—or sometimes kills—the fish. Fishers catch the

▲ Coral reefs are harmed when pieces are broken off for souvenirs.

stunned fish in their nets and sell them to fish dealers. The dealers then sell the fish to restaurants and pet stores. People often do not know the brutal way these fish were caught.

▲ Divers collect trash during a "Reef Relief" clean-up in Florida.

Today, some countries are trying to stop cyanide fishing. But the reefs still need protection. People continue to damage them in other ways. Maybe they will see the beauty of the coral reefs and stop before it is too late.

Glossary

algae—tiny plants that live in water

atoll—a ring-shaped coral reef in the open sea

barrier reef—a coral reef several miles from shore that creates a barrier between the land and the sea

budding—the process of a little bump forming on a polyp, growing larger, and becoming a new polyp

coral reefs—underwater structures formed by animals

equator—an imaginary line around the middle of the Earth

fringing reef—a coral reef that extends from the shore into the sea

polyps—small, soft coral animals

symbiosis—a relationship between two living things that benefits both members

tentacles—long, flexible structures at the mouth or head of an animal

zooplankton—tiny animals in the coral reef

- Coral animals need a hard surface to grow on. Some grow on underwater mountains and volcanoes.

- Some polyps are as long as 1 foot (30 centimeters).

- More than 80 percent of the coral reefs in the United States are in Hawaii.

- It is estimated that coral reefs support about 25 percent of all the different kinds of ocean animals.

At a Glance

Location: Almost all the world's reefs lie near the equator.

Types of coral reefs: Fringing reef, barrier reef, atoll

Description: Underwater structures formed by animals in warm, shallow, and tropical seas

Common animals: Polyps, sponges, moray eels, crown-of-thorns starfish, sea anemones, crabs

Common plants: Algae

Want to Know More?

At the Library

Fowler, Allan. *It Could Still Be Coral*. Danbury Conn.: Children's Press, 1996.

Kalman, Bobbie, and Niki Walker. *Life in the Coral Reef*. New York: Crabtree, 1997.

Sayre, April Pulley. *Coral Reef*. New York: Twenty-First Century Books, 1996.

Wu, Norbert. *A City under the Sea: Life in a Coral Reef*. New York: Atheneum Books for Young Readers, 1996.

On the Web

Animal Bytes: Coral Reefs
http://www.seaworld.org/animal_bytes/coralab.html
For facts about coral reefs and links to preservation organizations

Corals and Coral Reefs
http://www.seaworld.org/coral_reefs/introcr.html
For information about how to grow your own coral

Through the Mail

The Nature Conservancy
Rescue the Reef Program
1815 North Lynn Street
Arlington, VA 22209
To find out more about preserving coral reefs

On the Road

The Florida Aquarium
701 Channelside Drive
Tampa, FL 33602
813/273-4000
To see a coral reef and its wildlife

Index

About the Author

Susan H. Gray holds bachelor's and master's degrees in zoology from the University of Arkansas in Fayetteville. She has taught classes in general biology, human anatomy, and physiology. She has also worked as a freshwater biologist and scientific illustrator. In her twenty years as a writer, Susan H. Gray has covered many topics and written a variety of science books for children.